VHERSES

A Celebration of Outstanding Women

J. Patrick Lewis

illustrated by Mark Summers

Creative Editions

Designed by Rita Marshall

Text copyright © 2005 J. Patrick Lewis. Illustrations copyright © 2005 Mark Summers. Published in 2005 by Creative Editions. 123 South Broad Street, Mankato, MN 56001 USA. Creative Editions is an imprint of The Creative Company. All rights reserved. No part of the contents of this book may be reproduced by any means without the written permission of the publisher. Printed in Italy. **Library of Congress Cataloging-in-Publication Data:** Lewis, J. Patrick. Vherses: a celebration of outstanding women / by J. Patrick Lewis; illustrated by Mark Summers. ISBN 1-56846-185-2. 1. Women—Juvenile poetry. 2. Children's poetry, American. I. Summers, Mark. II. Title. PS3562.E9465V47 2005   811'.54—dc22   2004058232
First Edition 5 4 3 2 1

For Beth and Leigh Ann, the most outstanding women in my book. J.P.L.
To the two special women in my life, Shawn and Sienna. M.S.

By the mid-1800s, most civilized cultures had established notions of what a woman could and could not be. Accepted was the fact that there were certain roles and pursuits available to women, and boundaries they could not cross. But in the next century and a half, a wave of female fighters, pioneers, and standard-setters rose up to expose these confines as myth.

A Celebration of Outstanding Women

Among the fighters were Fannie Lou Hamer, Eleanor Roosevelt, and Rachel Carson. Prominent in the ranks of pioneers were Emily Dickinson, Amelia Earhart, and Gertrude Ederle. And setting new standards in arts and athletics were such figures as Martha Graham, Ella Fitzgerald, and Venus and Serena Williams.

Through verse and illustration, the following pages consider beauty, strength, compassion, and other virtues, defining them with women and girls whose lives and legacies transformed—and continue to transform—all concepts of woman.

My Agile Loom

Spin one word into spun gold—
A task to take a week—
Duplicate the deed with other
Words you needn't speak

Quilt them to the page—with care—
Then put the sheet away—
Next to Encyclopedia
Of Eccentricity—

My agile loom unwinds my soul—
But awkward spins the thread
Of life—I live to weave a word—
And so am comforted.

Emily Dickinson American poet 1830–1886

It is remarkable that one of the world's greatest poets published only seven poems during her lifetime. Emily Dickinson's lifework would remain in attics for a later generation to discover. A shy and housebound recluse, she preferred distance to social intimacy; never availing herself of marriage or children. But reading books took her near and far, high and deep into an emotional world. Emily was also stirred by meeting one Reverend Charles Wadsworth, whom she greatly admired. When he departed for the West Coast, she poured out her heartsick feelings in poetry. Nature, too, afforded her a rich vein for verse. Read a Dickinson poem and be prepared to experience the same sense of "otherness" she herself must have felt all her life.

Eleanor Roosevelt American first lady & diplomat 1884–1962

Eleanor Roosevelt made her home in the White House, but she was much more than the First Lady, a role she was to change forever. Arguably, more than any other U.S. president's wife, her achievements and reputation very nearly rivaled her husband's. Despite her troubled marriage to Franklin Delano Roosevelt, this mother of six children (one died in infancy) became the good-will ambassador to the world. As a U.S. delegate to the United Nations from 1945 to 1953, she chaired the commission that drafted the Universal Declaration of Human Rights. She was the tireless voice of the voiceless, one of the twentieth century's most enduring standard bearers for justice.

You Learn By Living

Who showed the world the world itself
   Was awkward, shy and plain.
A high-born leader in a long,
   Low decade full of pain.

Poor farmers, blacks, homeless, the least
   Advantaged hoped to see,
Magnificently unarrayed,
   Pure human dignity.

A lady first, the great first lady
   Looked fear in the face,
And said, *There is no room for fear*
   When courage take its place.

Georgia O'Keeffe *American artist 1887–1986*

Unstill Life

Master of the shifting shape,
Botanical and desertscape,

Her orchid still lifes might have meant
To call to mind a continent

Of love. The space of Western skies
Is fixed in the longhorn's empty eyes.

Romantic vistas hum out loud
Beneath the mesa's patterned cloud.

She gave bleached bones and ancient skulls
More life than living animals

That haunt the still and soft light show
Of her beloved New Mexico.

What is it if it is not art
That turns the handle of the heart?

Mother of the Dance

Face white death mask
Mouth a slash of red
Cheekbones sculpted stone
She moves to move
Like something said
A phantom bending
Bone to bone
TREMBLE
spAsm
sudden
f
      a
           l
               l

Delirium
The glance
Stark fantasy
In angles called
The Mother of the Dance.

13 "I did not want it to be beautiful or fluid," Martha Graham once said. "I wanted it to be fraught with inner meaning, with excitement and surge." In 1916, inspired by dance, Graham enrolled in Los Angeles's newly opened Denishawn School, founded by the dancer Ruth St. Denis and her husband, Ted Shawn, to teach techniques of dance. Over eight years, as both a student and an instructor, Graham considered Denishawn both her inspiration and her home. Her contributions to dance rival Picasso's to painting and Stravinsky's to music. She taught America's greatest dancers—including Alvin Ailey, Twyla Tharp, and Merce Cunningham. In stage design, dance production, and experimentation, Martha Graham's name is synonymous with *haute couture*.

Solo

A quilt of fog. The airplane's
Altimeter was gone,
The wings were icing over.
Still, she flew on and on.

Destination? Paris
Is what she'd always planned,
But she landed in the meadows
Of grateful Ireland.

They hailed her Lady Lindy,
First Lady of the Air,
First woman the Atlantic
Allowed to beat the dare.

Years later she's still missing
For what was meant to be—
Around-the-world Amelia—
Remains a mystery.

Amelia Earhart American aviatrix 1897–1937

After taking a $1, ten-minute plane ride at an airplane stunt show, Amelia Earhart knew she must learn to fly. She took lessons and, at the age of twenty-five, bought a plane of her own. After a 1928 transatlantic flight as a passenger, she set out to duplicate the feat singlehandedly. On May 20–21, 1932, Amelia crossed the Atlantic, establishing a new record of 13 hours, 30 minutes. She was widely celebrated throughout Europe and the United States. Five years later, Amelia began what was to be her final flight. She and her navigator, Fred Noonan, aimed to fly around the world in a twin-engine Lockheed Electra, but the U.S. Coast Guard lost contact with the plane over the South Pacific. The many theories of her disappearance have never been confirmed.

Anne Morrow Lindbergh Aviation pioneer & author 1906–2001

The Steep Ascent

She flew with him to farther stars
And reminisced in blithe memoirs
Of carefree youth. One tragic day
Her son was spirited away.

No one expects us to withstand
Pure evil with the upper hand,
But Time, wry keeper of our lives,
Taught her a certainty survives:

The terror when the living shed
Their hours of gold for hours of lead
Becomes, like her chaste pedigree,
A casual, worn nobility.

Rachel Carson *Marine biologist & environmentalist 1907–1964*

I Was Trying to Save the Beauty
of the Living World

Goliaths roar against her little book
Of secret ways those giants spoil the sea,
The flora, fauna . . . Everywhere you look—
Grim legacies of greed and gluttony.
Imagine then the atmosphere that shook
A world awake to nature's tragedy—
One woman with a mighty brief to bring
Against those who would destroy the rights of Spring.

Always a writer, Rachel Carson published her first piece at the age of ten in *St. Nicholas*, the children's magazine. A devotee of birds, animals, and nature of all kinds, this shy and unaffected loner was to loom larger than life in the way humans treated the planet. In 1951, her book *The Sea Around Us*, rejected by fifteen publishers, was finally accepted. It won the National Book Award and propelled Carson to international fame. But it was her later book, *The Silent Spring*, which placed her in the pantheon of environmental activists. Her determination to enlighten the world about the dangers to humankind of pesticides, such as DDT, heptachlor, and malathion, enraged their makers. Corporations vilified her as "that hysterical woman," but truth won out. She raised an awareness of our fragile planet like no one else had ever done before.

I'm Sick and Tired of Bein' Sick and Tired

This life was cottoncottoncotton
For me, my mother's twentieth child.
Plantations may be long forgotten
But not by folks they had defiled,

Freedom calls!
Plantation walls
Are made of sticks and stones and mud.
The hand that beats,
The man that mauls
To steal the soul will stir the blood.

She murmured, "Cotton,"
As she perspired,
"I'm sick and tired
Of bein' sick and tired."

Freedom yells!
But jail cells
Are meant to torture and to maim,
Those Mississippi
Citadels
Where Warden Scorn met Master Shame.

She whispered, "Cotton,"
As she perspired,
"I'm sick and tired
Of bein' sick and tired."

Freedom cries!
But in those eyes
An accusation will begin—
For what I did?
No, they despise
Me for the color of my skin.

She shouted, "Cotton,"
As she perspired,
"I'm sick and tired
Of bein' sick and tired."

The last of twenty children of Mississippi sharecroppers, Fannie Lou Hamer picked cotton from the age of six to help her family. "By the time I was thirteen," she said, "I was picking two and three hundred pounds." She dropped out of school after sixth grade but went on to become one of the nation's leading advocates for voting rights and spoke out against poverty. In 1963, during a civil rights trip to South Carolina, the bus in which she was riding stopped in Winona, Mississippi. Hamer and her co-workers went into the "white only" waiting room and were arrested and beaten unmercifully. Her injuries stayed with her for the rest of her life, but they emboldened her spirit and her commitment to justice.

Ella Fitzgerald American jazz singer 1918–1996

"I've Got You Under My Skin" was the name of one of the many Cole Porter tunes recorded by the supremely gifted Ella Fitzgerald. Read what some of her contemporaries have said about her: "I never knew how good our songs were until I heard Ella Fitzgerald sing them." (Ira Gershwin) "Her recordings will live forever." (Tony Bennett) "She was the best singer on the planet." (Mel Torme). Little is known about her youth, but in 1934, at the age of sixteen, Fitzgerald appeared on the stage of New York's Apollo Theater. From then on, she sang with the best orchestras in the land. Her astonishing diversity, in both range and style, included swing, bebop, scat, and jazz, as well as classics, blues, bossanova, gospel, calypso, and Christmas hymns. Despite countless awards and accolades, she maintained her graciousness and amazement at the love and affection from her worldwide audiences.

I've Got You Under My Skin

Left heaven on a holiday
Lived way down Memory Lane
Laughed hi-de-ho to heartache
Low shoo-be-doo to pain

Looped syllables in satin
Like bebop, jazz and scat
Left sitting high and handsome
"The Way You Wear Your Hat"

Lady for lonely evenings
Last sugar on the spoon
Like ear candy at midnight
Left all of us too soon

Swim, Girl, Swim

As Europe woke from sleep,   Many had tried to make
Young Trudy Ederle   This superhuman swim—
At Cap Gris Nez in France   Thirty-five punishing miles.
Dived into a daunting sea.   Chances, at best, were slim.

Gertrude Ederle American swimmer 1906–2003

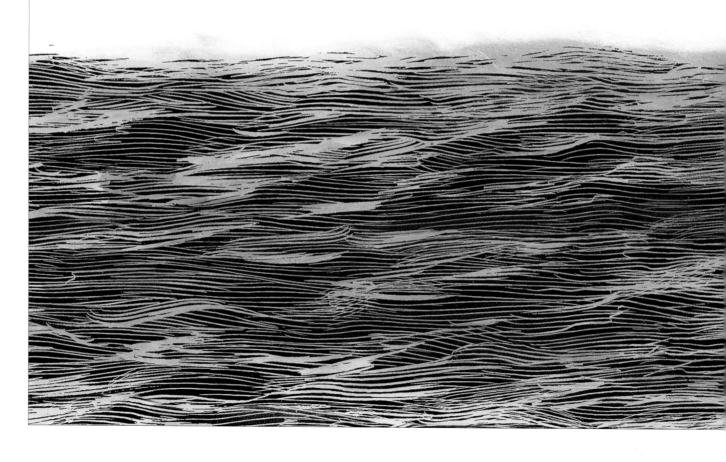

When Fury found the waves,
Far from the western shore,
Her trainer shouted, "Let's turn back!"
But Trudy cried, "What for?"

Under an English moon,
The celebration began
After the fastest crossing
By woman or by man.

"Swim, Girl, Swim" was the name of a movie based on Gertrude Ederle's achievement. As an eight-year-old visiting her grandmother in Germany, Gertrude tumbled into a pond and nearly drowned. Frightened but indomitable, she practiced swimming relentlessly. In 1925, the nineteen-year-old New Yorker came within seven miles of swimming the English Channel. A year later, London bookies gave 5–1 odds that she would fail again. But in August 1926, fighting rain, twenty-foot waves, jellyfish, and a numb left leg, she became the first woman to swim the Channel, and in a time—14 hours, 31 minutes—that beat the men's mark by nearly two hours and remained the women's record for thirty-five years.

Anne Frank Diarist 1929–1945

"People are really good at heart": so said an Amsterdam schoolgirl by the name of Anne Frank. In June 1942, Anne received a present on her thirteenth birthday—a small clothbound diary. Several weeks later, she and her family went into hiding on the upper floor of a warehouse annex, where they would remain virtually imprisoned by the Nazis for more than two years. Personalizing her diary as her friend, Anne named it "Kitty" and confided to it a candid portrayal of people threatened with imminent death and an examination of universal moral issues. *The Diary of Anne Frank* provides a lasting look at the extremes of degradation and nobility of the human spirit. She died of typhoid fever in the Bergen-Belsen concentration camp in March 1945, just two months before the German surrender.

People Are Really Good At Heart

Is there enough to eat, Father?
Is this a living tomb?
Can Hatred be so dark, Father,
It seals up a room?

Can you imagine now, Mother,
The girl I want to be?
I will not dream the dreams, Mother,
They'd take away from me.

We must be very quiet, Sister.
The annex walls are thin.
If nights like these should end, Sister,
When will our lives begin?

If Hatred walks the street, God,
And Death, the avenue,
Will Hatred walk with Death, God,
Because I am a Jew?

Jane Goodall British zoologist 1934–

Notes From a Day in the Bush

Continued to observe the troop at dawn:
How Fifi deftly navigates a limb,
Intently watching Flossi do vaudeville.
Morning breaks on David Graybeard's yawn.
Prof licks a stick, as I sit next to him,
Attempting to fish termites from a hill.
Nature is a strange phenomenon,
Zoology without the zoo. Call me,
Engaged upon a quest, a marathon
Eyewitness to a high society.

Anyone listening to a lecture by Jane Goodall, the most well-known animal behaviorist in the world, is in for a surprise. Somewhere along the way, she will let loose with the booming hoot of the chimpanzee, a refrain that punctuates life in the Tanzanian forests. Encouraged long ago by her mentor, Louis Leakey, Goodall took to the Gombe game preserve in Africa and sat still, listening, observing, befriending, and writing about chimpanzees for nearly thirty years. Her mission has been to answer the question: "How far along our human path, which has led to hatred and evil and full-scale war, have chimpanzees traveled?" Gremlin, Goliath, Goblin, Figan, Frodo, Little Bee, her favorite David Graybeard, and scores of other chimps have provided many answers.

Serena Williams Professional tennis star 1981–

Venus Williams Professional tennis star 1980~

Double Doubles [A Verse Served Up By Two Booming Voices]

I took the name
between the Earth
and Mercury.
We took our game
to beaded stars above.
My sister's

volleys
so astonish me,
the score

plenty–

where she'll be going.
We move together

The Williams sisters
read each other better

and everything between.
Momentum

the final tie-break.
Match point is only one

I know why
double doubles
players play.

We took our game
to beaded stars above.
My sister's
lobs and

so astonish me,

our score
is usually
plenty–
love.
I play as if I know

We move together
like a fine machine.
The Williams sisters

than _a_ to _z_

Momentum
takes us to

Match point is only one
quick ace away.
As soon as I see sister
Venus rising,

double doubles
players play.

The sports world has never seen anything quite like the Venus and Serena Williams phenomenon. Driven by their notoriously outspoken father, Richard, the Williams sisters took to tennis at the age of six and never looked back. Their father dubbed them "the next two female Michael Jordans," and they proved him right. In 1999, they won the French Open, becoming the first sisters to win a doubles title in the twentieth century. A year later, they claimed Olympic gold in Sydney. Venus captured Wimbledon's Women's Singles titles in 2000 and 2001, only to be defeated by Serena in the 2002 and 2003 championship matches. As the sisters' star continues to rise, they are likely to remain fixtures in the world of sports for years to come.